Juice

Poems by Nadia Arioli

Luchador Press
Big Tuna, TX

Copyright © Nadia Arioli, 2021
First edition 1 3 5 7 9 10 8 6 4 2
ISBN: 978-1-952411-51-9
LCCN: 2021931576

Cover image: Taylor Denise Teachout:
taylorteachout@yahoo.com
Author photo: Nadia Arioli
All rights reserved. No part of this publication may be reproduced or transmitted in any form or by any means, electronic or mechanical, including photocopying, recording or by info retrieval system, without prior written permission from the author.

Acknowledgments:

"Carrot," "Guava," "Horchata" appeared in *Bateau 9.1*.
"Vegetable" and "Lemon" appeared in *McNeese Review*.
"Carrot", "Grape", "Aloe Vera", and "Guava" appeared online at *PhilosophicalIdiot.Com*.

TABLE OF CONTENTS

Apple / 1

Beet / 3

Grapefruit / 5

Pomegranate / 7

Banana / 9

Hawaiian Punch / 11

Kool-Aid / 13

Mango / 15

Carrot / 17

Blueberry / 19

Limeade / 21

Unknown / 23

Cranberry / 24

Pineapple / 26

Coconut / 28

Cherry / 30

Grape / 31

Aloe Vera / 33

Lemonade / 35

Orange / 37

Vegetable / 39

Jungle Juice / 41

Milk / 43

Lemon / 45

Peach / 46

Pear / 48

Horchata / 49

Prune / 51

Guava / 53

Tomato / 55

Juice

Apple

Now seems like a good time to talk to you about apple juice.
Apple juice is a bullshit juice.
It looks like pee and will make you pee
an uncommon amount.
There is no time or place for apple juice,
unless you're a child, in which case,
why are you reading this? and your hands are the worst.
It's pure sugar,
and not in the fun way.
It is the smarm of juices.

However, add carbonation and a fun bottle
and oh shit! it's Martinelli's.
Champagne of the gods.
Light, refreshing, perfect for summer and fall.
Serve in a wine glass.
It does not look like pee,
unless you're much better about hydration than I am.

I got carded once buying Martinelli's.
I felt so sophisticated, so grown up.

On several occasions, I bullied my friends into taking shots of it
    with me,
and I regret nothing.

Apple cider is pretty good too, hot or cold.
The spice off-sets the sweetness,
which is how I like my women, too.

Since apple juice is the base of these amazing beverages,
it means all juice is beautiful and great,
even the ones that seem like bullshit.
Juice.

Beet

Now is a good time to talk to you about beet juice.
It's horrible. It tastes like musty carrot and a used tampon,
not in a good way. It tastes like a mistake.
It tastes like kissing the wrong person,
right on the mouth and with tongue.

I bought some on a whim today,
and it was the most Dallas Metroplex experience.
I had been rear-ended hard the day before
and was mad about traffic existing.
During rush hour, I decided to take a break,
and stopped at a juice place.

I'm not sure why I went with beet juice.
Trying something new, I guess,
or something that's supposed to be good for you.
It felt like "self-care" in a way people use that phrase
but don't actually know what it means.

I sat outside on a bench outside, grimacing my way through.
I refuse to waste $6 juice.

I was in a shopping strip that has places you can go if you're in
    suburban wasteland
and want to feel fancy and like you're living a good life.
Little boutiques and a pho place.
Places that aren't chains but might as well be.

I put on my yellow beanie. I don't know why.
It makes me look ridiculous and dumb.
I guess I wanted to remain anonymous, somehow.
People were looking at their cell phones anyways.

As I threw out the bottle, I heard, in the trees,
the deafening screams of hundreds of grackles.
The birds had nothing to do with me.
There, loud and clear, but somehow subsumed in the white
    noise,
a flock of grackles, shaking the tree.
Juice.

Grapefruit

Now is a great time to tell you about grapefruit juice.
It tastes like a snarky sunset.
Unlike orange juice or limeade,
it really does need to be fresh squeezed to be good.

Juicing a grapefruit is work for me.
I'm clumsy and don't handle knives well.
Furthermore, in the spring, my hands get eczema,
which seems to have spread to my face this year.
It's a sexy skin condition involving red bumps and peeling open,
the underripe skin pink like grapefruit.

It's not the pain that scares me but the potential for disappointment.
I'm lazy, sure, but mostly the risk.
If you don't put a lot of work into your art, your relationships,
exist as a typo,
you get walk away and say
"Don't think twice; it's alright. We never did too much talking anyways."

The labor of grapefruit juice makes it a gamble.
Will it be worth it?

I took a grapefruit and cut it in half.
My fingers stung just from being near.
Flesh on flesh.
I made the smallest glass for someone
who is accustomed to juice by the bottle.
No one knew.
I sipped.
Tasted like victory.
Juice.

Pomegranate

Now is a great time to talk about pomegranate juice.
The color alone is a thing of beauty:
red with notes of purple, like an anger going out.
The flavor is apples and flowers and cinnamon
and a meadow, somewhere, that you can go to when you
    need it.

The problem is, it's expensive as fuck.
I don't think it's necessarily that overpriced,
considering the amount that must go into making it:
undoing the skin, picking beads out of honeycomb, and
    straining the seeds.
I don't have that kind of money right now.

And even if I did, would I?
I've been reading a lot about imposter syndrome lately,
and it almost fits. I almost feel like I'm faking it
and don't deserve nice things, even the ones I've worked for.

I say "almost,"
because it's imposter syndrome all the way down.

I'll light my house on fire and crash my new car.
I'll tear off all my skin in a fit of eczemic rage.
The blood will peek through in drops like seeds.

Except not.
I'm nowhere near that thrilling.
Most pomegranate juice is mostly apple anyways, if you look at the ingredients.
Juice.

Banana

Now is a good time to talk about banana juice.
You said it was your favorite.
You say a lot of things. You are noisesome
in the most comforting of ways.
I looked for it at the store the other day,
and the closest I came was strawberry banana,
and it was delicious as heck.

It's thick and sweet
(which, as we've discussed, is how I like my women).
It's filling and comforting and good right before brushing
    your teeth.
I fucked up the order last night, but you know what?
It was still okay.

But what I like about it most is the color.
Pink and yellow. Rose pink. Subdued.

The color reminds me of my complex relationship to my
    gender.
I identify as a woman, but not like that.
I feel sexy when half my hair is buzzed.

Children make me uncomfortable. I cuss. I am often lewd.
I rarely wear make-up.

We live in better times now, where identifying as non-binary
is a beautiful and valid option.
I looked at the Catholic mothers in my community,
and I looked at myself.
I am still a woman, but not like that.
Pink but yellow, subdued.

A year ago, America elected Trump.
Pussy grabs back.
I'm grabbing back with chewed up fingernails
and all the rage of a banana juice samurai.
Juice.

Hawaiian Punch

Now is a good time to tell you about Hawaiian Punch.
What is it, anyways? I think it's supposed to be mango and
    pineapple,
but most people know it as having the flavor that is Red.

College students only use it as a vehicle for vodka and
    Everclear,
but that is where they are wrong.
I've certainly had my share of trashcan punch and shitshow
    adventures,
back when I used to drink.

What I miss about alcohol is the ability to relax my spine.
Despite having friends, I always feel like an outsider looking in.
I don't pity myself for this, just acknowledge that is the way
    I am.
Drop me in any social situation, and that is the case.
I made eye-contact once in 2011, and it was devastating.
I feel like I'm making home movies for the folks back home.
Alcohol helped.

I grew more affectionate with each sip.
I could offer a firm handshake or a slap on the back and declare
    my love, like "Good for you, sport."
So affection is not my strong suit.

But alcohol felt forced and hysterical and fake
so I all-but gave it up. Hawaiian Punch, on the other hand,
never told lies it thought you would believe.
It never pretended it had nutritional value. It tastes Red.

Once, at a party, I danced.
"King Kunta" was playing, and I got down.
My friends were shocked and asked what I was drinking.
I said "Nothing but Hawaiian Punch, man."
Juice.

Kool-Aid

Now is a good day to tell you about Kool-Aid.
Like most people who grew up in a cult,
I've only drunk it one memorable time.
And let me tell you, it is some bullshit not-quite juice.

It's basically Fun Sticks,
which is a cocainy candy,
and has nothing to do at all with fruit
or something that grew in dirt.

To add insult to injury, the Kool-Aid packet instructions
    state to add sugar.
So is this shit instant or not?
Like, I don't mind juice I got to work for—I squeezed
grapefruit by hand, the pulp and juice a bloody triumph—
and instant powder drinks like Tang can be great, but not
    this in- between bullshit.

I am a person of extreme beliefs when it comes to juice
    and God.

The cult was praying in tongues and getting slain in the spirit
and hell and angels.
My new-found atheism is blank and white,
like a pile of sugar
that doesn't need something prepackaged and dyed and
 forced on children
to feel like it works.
Juice.

Mango

Now is a great time to talk to you about mango juice.
It is sunshine, it is paradise.
And I don't mean that place you may or may not go to when
    you die for being good;
I just mean a little respite,
in a can or bottle.

"Being good" is a sticky phrase when it comes to women,
I think. They say "Well-behaved women rarely make
    history"
but even then, they still want you to conform to some
    image.
I am Wonder Woman.
I am a virgin whore.

I remember being in a crowd of men at a bar,
and one said to another "You can't tell her what to do,"
meaning me, as if I were a child.

I am curves,
but that doesn't mean sex.

I am smooth,
but don't fucking touch me.
I am exhausted from whispering "Me too."
Do I not deserve respite?

And at my center is a core you will never see.
You don't care about that.
You want sweet in convenient packaging.
You're afraid if you find that center, you'll choke.
Juice.

Carrot

Now is a good time to talk to you about carrot juice.
The flavor is so complex.
Like the first bite of an apple or caramel mixed with stew.
Sweet in a way that feels odd,
although sweetness in carrot is not unprecedented,
such as carrots broiled with brown sugar or carrot cake.

I regard it with trepidation.
The flavor defies a solid description.
Moreover, drinking carrot juice feels so deliberate
and kind a thing to do to one's body.

I find it more natural and befitting
when something grotesque happens to mine.
Always, but especially after my body betrayed me
while being raped
or ended a life that never was.

I enjoy getting zits the size of hotels on my shoulders.
When my friend got an eye-infection,
I got jealous.

A boy who used to flirt with me told me
that if I were the size I am now when I was in college,
he would have never paid attention to me.
I wished I had eaten nothing but cake for years
before I had the misfortune of meeting him.

My boyfriend likes to go on walks with me.
Doing this feels kind to him,
and I can forget about my body,
except for my hand in his.
The leaves are gathering on the sidewalks,
and one is all the way caramel,
except for a splash of orange in the center.
Juice.

Blueberry

Now feels like a good time to talk to you about blueberry juice.
This part is urgent because most Americans
don't even know what that is.
You're probably thinking something like "syrup" or "cough medicine,"
and you're not entirely wrong.

But in Italy, you can get these little bottles
filled with the stuff at Dem, and it's actually quite refreshing.

One other person in my class enjoyed the 6-ounce bottles of blueberry juice,
and we talked about in our way to the visa office.
He told me to try to blackberry juice too by the same brand.
I'm not great at talking to folks, especially if they're also awkward,
but I can talk to anyone about the wonders of juice.

Later, this fellow juice connoisseur wandered off campus
in the middle of the night to try and join a monastery.
He packed his bags and disappeared.

He wandered back on campus the next day, and his dad
    flew out to get him,
and I haven't heard from him since.

I think losing your mind when you're a student
studying abroad is pretty common.
Something about being young, in a new place, religion,
and the liberal arts. I don't know.
But it happened to me too.

I don't know where to get blueberry juice, but if I did,
I'm not sure I would drink it without a great deal of caution.
The past can get sticky, and there is no known medicine for that.
Juice.

Limeade

Now is a good day to talk to you about limeade.
Dan insists that it is the drink of the summer.
I'm squarely in the lemonade camp,
but I do see his point.
Something about that sour and sweet
and the inevitable puckering of the lips
has to do with the heat and days of uninterrupted freedom
    as a child.

If you want a good limeade, go to Braum's.
A sad-day meal for me is fries, fried chicken club, and a
    limeade.
Braum's leaves the lime in the beverage,
and it floats around like a friendly millipede.

It's super sweet and super sour.
It packs a punch for something non-alcoholic
and in Styrofoam.
It tastes like candy
and the sad parts of childhood you still are nostalgic for.

I try to limit my sad-day meals.
You can't pretend food is a good listener.
But every year, mid- spring, I go and get my sad-day meal with my best friend.
Anniversary Effect is too goddamn real.
It makes my face get schrunchy
and leaves my mouth with the strangest of tastes.
Juice.

Unknown

Today is a great day to tell you about an unknown juice.
I gave it to you in the hospital
when I was made out of cardboard.
I said "Oh wow you really like juice too."
Wish like hell I could remember what it was.
Juice.

Cranberry

I'm going to talk to you about cranberry juice today too.
This one might take a while to get down to the point, if there
    is one.
Let me start by saying that it's fall, and also four years ago,
I took home Peter, my orange tabby.

Some weeks later, Margaret posted a picture of the found-cat
    posters Katie had put up
and asked "Hey, isn't this your cat Apollo?" to Andrew and
    Emma.
I thought "Oh fuck. I accidentally stole a cat.
I don't want to give him up. He's my very best friend."
So I texted Andrew. "Hello. I stole your cat, and I neutered him.
What should I do."
Andrew replied "Hello, ball stealer! Also, who is this?".
He let me keep the cat.

A month later, I ran into Andrew at Tom Thumb,
and we were both wearing orange sweaters.
I said I was buying stuff for Thanksgiving,
but I had put the cranberries in the bottom of the basket,
and they're probably crushed by now.

Andrew said the berries are fine,
they're tough, you know.

Unlike the popular juice beverage,
the berries are so sour and sting like a stingy piss,
in a good and satisfying way.
They don't go down easy,
unlike a juice cocktail laden with sugar.

I prefer the juice to the berries, to be honest.
I like it when things are easy
and can be consumed in large quantities.

But there's only one cat named Peter
who used to torment Andrew,
and there was only one of him too.
When I get home from work and before I go to the
    art-gallery to drop off my work,
I will hug that cat. I will hug him a lot
Juice.

Pineapple

Now is a good time to talk to you about pineapple juice.
I was obsessed with it as a kid and in college.
I would buy cans of pineapple and slurp the juice out of the can,
not even bothering with a glass.
My mouth would be sore after, but in a good way.

Flesh stripped away can be pleasant.
The rawness. Feeling out cautiously, like everything is new.

It's hard for me to admit that.
I don't have OCD
(and proved it in a poem by repeating "I don't have OCD" eleven
 times)
but I picked up some of the tendencies through the family trait.
Once, in a fit of anxiety, I had to leave class and finish peeling
off an entire fingernail because it wasn't quite right.
The hollow looked like a mouth.
I didn't have a band-aid
and had to slurp up the mess.

People never peg me for that,
for obsessing and being compelled,

due to my natural messiness,
inclination towards typos, and nonchalant approach to
  appearance.

It's gotten a lot better.
Learning not to eat away at myself.
I started reading in chapters instead of eleven-page segments
(rounding up to 100 when I hit 99, otherwise that would be
  cuckoo bananas).
And maybe it sounds dumb, but I am super proud of myself.

Pineapple juice isn't dangerous, per se.
You just have to be careful with it, lest it take away all feeling.
I ordered it at a bar once, and it came in a comically small can.
It was enough.
Juice.

Coconut

Now is a great time to talk to you about coconut juice.
Milk, water, it's fine.
It tastes like sheet cake.
It would be more refreshing if it weren't so sweet.
It makes my tongue and mouth itch if I have too much of it,
but it does make me feel fancy, which is appealing.

The main draw of coconut juice is, of course, the chewy chunks.
Coconut meat.
Pour it into a glass, and they even look like skin globs,
beyond just the texture.

I ate part of my mouth once, and it felt good.
It was during Christmas break when I was in college.
In front of my whole family, my dad had asked why I didn't receive Communion.
I mumbled something.

The thing was, I was an adult.
The thing was, I didn't believe in God,
but still thought what happened was a sin
because I must have subconsciously wanted it, right?

Late at night, I did something just for me and nobody else.
I sucked my lips in and bit until I tasted blood.
Chunks of me swam down my throat.
I am a shark, I thought. My mouth itched.
I don't recommend this course of private retaliation
against the people who make unreasonable demands of your
    mouth,
but I'd be lying if I said it didn't make me feel better.
Juice.

Cherry

Now is a good time to tell you about cherry juice.
It is only the flavoring that is horrible, not the thing itself.
I bought some today, for the first time.
The real thing, not flavored goo.
All black cherry. Organic.

It's good, soothing even, like blowing out a flame.
But I can't shake the feeling it's chapstick. Smackers.

It's associations that make healing things almost unbearable.
Take therapy, for example. I told my friend in jest that
it's like spelunking inside your own asshole.
It's all those flavors from childhood,
like being asked to give an account of yourself,
right at the forefront.

Once as kid, my dad and I went camping.
From the back seat, the wind chapped my lips to blood.
My dad scolded me for picking and asked why.
But he gave me his Vaseline because I didn't have anything.
It didn't taste like fruit. Bitter and medicinal.
It tasted like love.
Juice.

Grape

Now is a good time to tell you about grape juice.
You know you're at a weird stage of your adult life
when you feel too impure for grape juice.
Let me explain.
When I think of grape juice, I think of two things.

The first is childhood.
When we were kids, my mom would make my sisters and
    me grape juice
from concentrate and mix it with a big wooden spoon.
Red, but white grape if we were feeling fancy.
Sticky lips, our first terrible lipstick.
A blood-purple smear.
We would always make her make it,
even though it's simple enough for a kid.
I think it made us feel loved.

And she did love me, when I was easy to love,
a dopey kid who loved to read, back before puberty
(cotton underwear smeared purple red)
and before asking too many questions.

The second thing about grape juice is it makes me think of wine.
We were Catholics as well as being part of a cult, so we didn't
 fuck around.
We practiced with grape juice, though, practiced being a vessel
 for our Lord of Love.

My boyfriend make himself grape juice from concentrate
as I was leaving to drive home, because, hey, that shit is good.
I said I wasn't thirsty and left.
I cried a little driving home.
I miss my mom.
She was manipulative, told me her suicide-attempt was my fault,
 and disowned me,
and I miss her.
I miss going to Mass on All Souls' Day, and comfort in the
 feeling of a certain fate.
Juice.

Aloe Vera

Today is a good day to talk about Aloe Vera juice.
The drink is viscous and goes down in blobs.
The sweetness is hard to describe:
not like sugar or cane syrup but of a hard-won battle
    against the desert.

The cream, of course, is good for burns.
I like to imagine the juice is good for the insides.

They say the best way to heal yourself is through forgiveness,
and I must confess, I feel unsteady in my grasp of the
    concept.
Sure, you can talk to me about letting go,
of saying someone no longer has power over you.
But I don't know what that means on a pragmatic level.
It isn't smooth, whatever it is, and it takes big gulps to get
    it down.

Perhaps when someone says they're sorry, you don't have
    to forgive them.
Perhaps you can thank them instead.

It is a secret gift, born of a battle you don't get to see.

But what do I know? I'm still just a screwed-up kid in the juice
    aisle,
who says pretty things and should know more by now.
But, for what it's worth, I'm sorry too.
Juice.

Lemonade

Now feels like a good time to talk to you about lemonade.
You might be thinking that now is a strange time to speak
    of this fruit beverage,
as it is few days before Halloween, not summer,
which is when we think of lemonade,
as well as children being poisoned by capitalism at a young age.

But, listen, there are all kinds of lemonade in all kinds of
    places.
My very favorite is from Dave's Barbeque in south Dallas.
They say it's homemade but either way wouldn't surprise me.
It doesn't appear to be anything special, in the plastic cup,
and its chief ingredient is definitely sugar.

Perhaps it's the way it pairs with barbeque pork and sausage
that makes it so good. Cool and sweet against hot and tangy.

I got it to-go once and drank the whole dang thing
before I even made it home, and it's not a long drive if you
    go fast.
I was in a rush because I didn't want to miss the locksmith.

Two years ago, a few days before Halloween,
I had a locksmith come by my home. He asked me what I needed,
and I told him I was broke as fuck,
but I needed something that would hold and keep my ex-boyfriend out.
The locksmith said "Okay". Afterward, he gave me a bill for $345,
and said he took debit. It looked like my card went through.

I checked my bank statement a few weeks later to see how fucked I was.
The locksmith didn't charge me a dime.

Dave's is still open, but now with a different name, Bubba's.
Some sort of divorce dispute or something.
They kept the menu the same.
The lemonade is still as sweet.
Juice.

Orange Juice

Now feels like a good time to talk to you about orange juice.
I don't believe in the Platonic Forms, but if I did,
I would posit that orange juice is most like the Form of juice.
It is quintessential.

Fresh squeezed is best.
Like sunshine and vacation for your mouth.
Good with breakfast, obviously, but also with a nice salad,
    or on its own.

But shit orange juice
made from dehydrated oranges and chemicals is good too.
There's no substitute. From a bottle or crappy diner. Sour
    and gritty.

Once, years ago, Dan accidentally said he loved me
when he was saying goodbye at the airport.
I squeaked and got lost driving back.
When Dan got back from his vacation,
he said it on purpose, and I said it back.

Then I fled to his porch and had a glass of shitty orange juice
    and a Pall Mall.

Emotions are hard when you live like a snail in your own head.
Just as a snail is its own shell and lives in it, so too the barriers
    you make.

The Pall Mall was cheap.
The orange juice was prosaic at best.
But together, calm, peace.
Breathing and measured sips.
A masterpiece of ordinary.
Juice.

Vegetable

Today is a good day to talk to you about vegetable juice.
Here, I am referring to green mashed-up goodness,
such as, Naked's "Green Machine," although there are
    cheaper versions of the stuff.

You feel so wholesome.
You feel so good. Wow.
Half an apple and a pound of spinach all in this little bottle?
Drinking it feels like an act of self-love,
provided you don't look at the sugar content.

I got a knock-off version once, and it just wasn't the same.
My friend was coming over, and I needed refreshments.
I think it was "Bolthouse Farms."
The green was lighter, and it felt less thick,
and had a chalky after-taste I didn't like.

We discussed the matter at length.
The main thing was that note of jalapeño right at the end.
Unpleasant and startling and invasive.

Despite the juice, we had a good day, my friend and I.
When I was depressed, I had made a fort out of my two shitty
    couches
and attached a TV at one end with duct tape.
I was less depressed now, but I still had it up.
He was depressed that day
 (girl problems, if I had to guess)
but being in a nest with some weird juice seemed to help.

It's nice to be able to give what small, imperfect comforts you
have to someone that gets it.
He moved away some time ago,
but I hope he's getting plenty of interesting juices.
I'll make a point of seeing him, someday,
and face that wistfulness of how you change yourself entirely
but everyone else stays exactly as you remember them.
It'll sting, but only a little.
Juice.

Jungle

Now is a great time to talk to you about Jungle Juice.
You tell me it is your favorite,
and I confess to not knowing what it is.
You say it was the sort of thing that would come in school lunches.
Small cartons with animals on them.
You say you're not sure you could drink them now;
it's much too sweet.

Nothing could be more home-like than a school lunch.
Care and work and routine.
When I went to your house for the first time,
there were small sandwiches in a pile.
Cheese and turkey on white bread.
No wonder was they tasted so good.

Finding safe-spaces can be hard as a vagabond of a human.
I don't trust. I never stay too long.
I think perhaps I am a carton; cardboard no matter how much clawing.
Just layers of "Keep Out".

But, oh gosh, that porch and those nights.
And and and and.
They felt like a home for me,
for a few scattered hours at least.
And that will never be too sweet for me.
Juice.

Milk

Now is a good time to talk to you about milk.
When I first started talking about making a draft of this,
a friend wrote,
in a tone that I can only imagine as huffy,
"So you're not even going to write about milk?"
In your face, you fuck!

When I think of milk, there are obvious associations.
Childhood. Milk and cookies.
Santa. Purity in a glass.
And with that, certainty and safety.

But I'd like us to think about milk as a juice.
And I know that it may seem like a stretch,
but let us examine the concept of juice, for a moment.
Juice can be fruit, and juice can be vegetable.
Everyone agrees.
People would also agree that juice can be altered in some way,
adding in other ingredients, like sugar and water,
and then refrigerated.
What is grass, but a vegetable?

What is a cow, but a process whereby ingredients are altered?
Lactose is a type of sugar.
Milk is a kind of juice.
Cow juice, which sounds like broth,
which is another matter altogether,
and "broth" is a gross word anyways.

Milk is a juice, and don't you forget it.

A few months back, after a night of drinking and rooftop art shows,
we went to a stink breakfast at Judy's Cafe # 2.
An old lady yelled at our tattooed friend for wearing a dress.
His wife was loud. I was loud.
I referred to someone we all know as a cunt.
You ordered milk.

I laughed at you, then. But I think, perhaps you were on to something.
Taking what is coarse and from guts and making something wholesome and pure.
Giving yourself a new childhood, without ever needing Santa Claus.
Milk. I mean, juice. Juice.

Lemon

Today is a great day to talk to you about lemon juice.
And I don't mean lemonade, I mean the juice.
Straight from a lemon or from a bottle that looks like a lemon.

It is not refreshing in the least.
It is good for a sore throat or dare but not a whole lot else, on its own.

You're the only person I know who likes lemon juice,
and it feels right to me that you do.
You pass it off by saying you're a sour nut, and your candy stash confirms it.

You don't sugarcoat things and that makes you an optimist.
My work had a motivational speaker come in,
and when someone asked me what I thought,
I said I thought he was the Antichrist.

Because optimism is not about making things better.

It is not about saying let's make lemonade
when there is no sugar or water to be found.
It is about facing the sting and crying afterwards and
    choosing it anyways.
Juice.

Peach

Now is a great time to talk to you about peach juice.
It is the color of egg yolks, the sweetness of pie,
the light acid flavor of a cleaning solution.
It was not what I expected;
I expected texture and thickness.
Peaches, after all, are known for their fuzz
and being shaped like a nice bottom.
This was smooth and without residue.

When I got really sick two years ago,
I had expected texture and somethings to stick.
Like when I got sad before.
But this time, this time was just nothing.
I couldn't think in terms of concrete qualities.
I stopped sleeping and eating.
Puddlebrain. I felt nothing,
like I had swallowed bleach.

I have no advice of surviving a complete mental shut down,
other than avoiding Tao Lin.
The best thing I can tell you is to think about Lent.

How it's forty days of waiting and still and hush.
And then, then it'll stop one day.
Suddenly and slowly, somehow, like a sunrise.
It'll feel like Easter—
just not in the way you expected.
Juice.

Pear

Now feels like a good time to put in a word about pear
    juice.
I like my juice like I like my women:
think and sweet and with a bit of grit.
Refreshing and good any time of the day or night.
Try it with gin. Drink it by the gallon.
Will give you an extreme amount of energy.
You can do it. You can do anything.
Juice.

Horchata

Now is a great time to tell you about horchata.
It's rice juice, motherfucker.
Sweet and surgary and spicy.
The way it hits the back of your throat,
like quenching a thirst you didn't know you had.

When I think of horchata, I think of Christmas,
and I couldn't remember why.
We were an eggnog family, growing up.
Perhaps it's the way it's white and cold like snow.
Or the vanilla and cinnamon like cookies.
Spiked or not, it creates a warmth, spreading out from the chest,
a sort of hush, like a small bulb of light.

Dan made horchata last Christmas,
and this must be real reason I have that association.
He made a pitcher of it,
and there was great party of adult orphans gathered around it
in an apartment full of light.

Admitting that the holidays are hard is difficult
and implies a certain dissatisfaction at the way your life
    has turned out.
But that's not what I mean. I mean, around this time
    of year,
I start to miss the things I never had but still somehow lost.

I'll help make the horchata this year.
I'm an appalling chef, but it looks easy enough.
You gather and measure the ingredients.
The most important thing you can do wait.
Juice.

Prune

Now is a great day to talk to you about prune juice.
Truthfully, I think it's cursed, and I avoid it.
It looks like secrets and bile.
I've heard that Dr. Pepper is essentially carbonated prune juice,
and who the fuck wants flat Dr. Pepper?

I am trying to draw an arrow in my mind between prunes,
defecating, and pruning.
Getting rid of what is extra to make room in your stomach and
    in your life
for new growth.

The problem is knowing when to stop.
Fuck you, Marie Condo.

In dreams, my rib cage falls out my colon.
I feel like I push too far and not enough all at once.

I'm getting a new housemate next week,
and I'm a little nervous.

It will be six months of three adults living there.
But the house will fill up with redundant furniture
and noise and smells and clashing decoration.
Bohemian Squalor Kingdom, and I am the empress.
I don't need to purify a goddamn thing.
Juice.

Guava

Now is a great day to speak about guava juice.
Sweet and understated,
like finding an old notebook you thought you lost
or holding hands without even thinking.
Thick like breathing in yarn.

When you were a baby, you had asthma.
A breathing machine you cannot remember.
Of all the things your body could be bad at, it went with
    breathing.
And really, it was all downhill from there.
Pissing itself at night far too long out of sheer terror.
Blood that leaped out of veins.

A month ago, you went to Fort Worth Gardens with your
    boyfriend.
The path was wide enough for two so you could hold hands.
You walked liked it was the easiest thing in the world,
despite menstrual cramps forming.
You talked about moving with him and beds you would one
    day share.

Afterwards, you were thirsty,
so he pulled over into a 711 on the ride home.
Strangely, they have guava juice.
Pink and exotic in a world of Coca-Cola and Bud Lite.
You drink it all in the parking lot and sigh contentedly.
You are going to live. You are going to live forever.
Juice.

Tomato

Right now is the best time to talk about tomato juice.
Tomato juice is a bullshit juice.
Besides apple juice, this is the only other juice that is pure b.s.

The thing that gets me is the salt.
And I love salt. A fine mist over salad or fries.
Rocks of it on pretzels.
But in a beverage? It's just nonsense.
Juices are for quenching.

I think the reason a salty beverage offends me
is that I already have to drink more than my fair share of salt.
Not in the filthy way, just that I'm a cryer.

I wasn't always like this, I promise.
I think becoming a cryer happened around the same time
    I decided to be more open.
When my mom tried to kill herself,
I knew somehow that I had to make a choice: open or shut.

I don't do things that are in-between.
Which is why I find tomato juice to be some fucking shit.
Is it cold soup? Will make me stop wanting?

And I guess at this point I seem wildly unbalanced and
    unstable.
Too open and rambling,
like something that spilled and can't be put back.
But I'm still hiding and without a visible list of ingredients.
Because if you talk to anyone about anything and everything
in the juice aisle at Wholefoods,
they'll never know the real reason why you're crying.
Juice.

Nadia Arioli (nee Wolnisty) is the founder and editor in chief of *Thimble Literary Magazine*. Their work has appeared or is forthcoming in *Spry, SWWIM, Apogee, Penn Review, McNeese Review, Kissing Dynamite, Bateau, Heavy Feather Review, Whale Road Review, SOFTBLOW*, and others. They have chapbooks from Cringe-Worthy Poetry Collective, Dancing Girl Press, and Spartan Press.

www.ingramcontent.com/pod-product-compliance
Lightning Source LLC
Chambersburg PA
CBHW030351100526
44592CB00010B/918